The Song
of
Songs

The Song of Songs

according to the translation
of King James

ILLUSTRATED WITH WOODCUTS BY
Cecil Buller

AND WITH AN AFTERWORD BY HER SON
Dr Sean B Murphy

Fomorian Press
Ottawa
2001

Published by
Fomorian Press
471 Athlone Avenue
Ottawa, Ontario
K1Z 5M9

Telephone: (613) 728–5587
Facsimile: (613) 728–9754
Electronic mail: baddog@cyberus.ca

ISBN 1-894083-08-3

Contents

How This Book Came to Be

The Book

THE SONG OF SONGS IS A MYSTERIOUS BOOK. IT STANDS OUT AS UNIQUE IN the array of ancient texts that make up *The Bible*, and over the centuries, many people have wrestled with the question of why it is there.

The Song of Songs is not a part of the *Apocrypha*, the body of disputed books of the *Bible*. It appears in every version of the *Bible*, in much the same form, although not in the same place in all versions. It is variously known as the *Song of Songs*, the *Song of Solomon* (King Solomon, 961–922 BC, is traditionally cited as the author) and the *Canticle of Canticles*.

On its face, the *Song* is a love poem of richly erotic imagery, in the form of a dialogue between King Solomon and the daughter of the Pharaoh of Egypt as they woo one another, with a chorus of courtiers or friends in the background.

Its idiom is frankly sensual, and quite discordant with the rest of the *Bible*. In consequence, many people have felt a need to interpret the *Song* allegorically. A metaphor for God's love for the Christian Church (even though it was written perhaps a thousand years before the founding of the Christian religion) is a popular, but by no means the only, Christian interpretation. One wonders why the author would have gone into such detailed description simply to get this point across! It has also been the subject of a number of interpretations that advocate an ascetic way of life, which some readers may find ironic.

The tone of the work is very reminiscent of the courtly love poems of the Middle Ages. Appropriately, it is said to have been the Biblical book most frequently interpreted in the Mediæval period, by both Christians and Jews.

The *Song* was interpreted in 1931 in a series of highly sensual woodcuts by Cecil Buller, a Canadian artist then living in Paris. The cuts were published along with a French version of the text by Isaac de Maistre de Sacy under the title *Cantique des cantiques.*

One of the questions that arose in the course of production of the present edition was what text of the *Song of Songs* to use. We eventually chose the King James version. The language is graceful, and the text is familiar to many people, although regrettably to fewer each year.

While consideration was given to using the French text, it was eventually decided that it would unduly restrict access to the book by English-speaking readers. Certainly if we were to publish a French edition, we would restore Maistre de Sacy's text.

The Woodcuts

The history of Ms Buller's book is recounted by her son, Dr Sean Murphy, in a reminiscence that appears at the back of the present work.

Maria Tippett, in *By a Lady*, her study of the under-representation of women among famous Canadian artists, alluded to Cecil Buller's work as an example, and reproduced one woodcut from the *Cantique des cantiques* series. The designer of the present edition was so struck by the one cut that he sought out the series and, having seen it, resolved to republish.

The order of the cuts as they appear here is somewhat different from that of the 1931 edition. John J.A. Murphy, Cecil Buller's husband and the book designer of *Cantique des cantiques*, arranged the cuts out of sequence with the story, most as tailpieces to the eight chapters. As Dr Sean Murphy notes, the cut that appears on page 12 of the present edition was the final illustration of the 1931 edition. That picture, unique in its tone and in the location it portrays, was a particularly satisfying picture to end on. John Murphy's arrangement gives the book a strong formal balance. We have chosen to group the cuts no more than a page away from the verses they illustrate, allowing the reader to savour them in the context of the poem.

The Type

The tropical lushness of Cecil Buller's interpretation of the *Song* is in sharp contrast to the cool modern lines of the then new *Futura* typeface (Paul Renner, 1927) in which *Cantique des cantiques* was set by her husband. No doubt at the time the book appeared, the style of the type and the woodcuts combined to give the book a novel appearance. *Cantique* was no doubt a fine and innovative example of the book designer's art.

But the designer of this edition felt that the warmth of the woodcuts would be better presented to a modern audience in a calligraphic text setting. He attended a typographic convention in Toronto in 1996, at which AGFA Canada was introducing a digital revival of Carl Dair's *Cartier* typeface. AGFA very kindly provided an advance copy of *Cartier*. The typeface was an excellent complement to Buller's woodcuts, and work was begun on the new edition of *The Song of Songs*.

Carl Dair, a Toronto graphic artist (b Welland, Ontario, 1912) was commissioned by the Government of Canada in 1957 at the urging of the then Head of the National Gallery of Canada, Alan Jarvis, to create a Canadian typeface to be used in publications for the 1967 Centennial of Confederation.

Dair was sent to apprentice as a type designer at Joh. Enschedé en zonen in Haarlem, the Netherlands, on a Canadian Government Overseas Award. But he was unable to complete the assignment until Centennial Year itself, by which time it was too late to produce and use the font. Dair, who had been in ill health for some time, died within a year, and the type effectively disappeared from sight. Some sketches and finished drawings are on display in the Robertson Davies Library print shop at Massey College, University of Toronto. Dair designed a roman and an italic style of his type. The uppercase letters were the same for both styles. There were no bold variants.

Cartier was the first Canadian-designed typeface since Methodist missionary James Evans designed a font for a Cree syllabary in 1841 to print a Cree spelling book. (Evans had been prevented by the Hudson's Bay Company from importing proper supplies to manufacture the type, probably because the Company feared relinquishing its monopoly on communication with the natives. He secretly cast a fount from the lead linings of tea chests and mixed lampblack and whale oil to produce the ink. Birchbark substituted for paper.)

A Historic Revival

The *Cantique des cantiques* series of prints was Cecil Buller's masterwork. Fomorian Press is pleased to make these woodcuts more readily available to the Canadian public nearly 70 years after they were created. It is our hope that this book will be a historical record of an important work of Canadian fine art, and that both text and illustrations will provide readers with many years of pleasure.

Acknowledgements

The publisher wishes to thank the following people and institutions: Dr *Sean B Murphy*, Ms Buller's son, very kindly lent the original woodcuts from which the illustrations for this book were scanned, and has given advice and support throughout the project.

The *National Library* helped with the initial research for this book, and the *National Gallery of Canada* provided study prints that aided in the design process. Special thanks to Rosemarie Tovell, the Gallery's Associate Curator, Canadian Prints and Drawings, for her encouragement.

AGFA *Canada* provided the type.

Until the day break,
and the shadows flee away.

The song of songs, which is Solomon's.

1

THE SONG OF SONGS, WHICH IS SOLOMON'S.

1:2 Let him kiss me with the kisses of his mouth: for thy love is better than wine.

1:3 Because of the savour of thy good ointments thy name is as ointment poured forth, therefore do the virgins love thee.

1:4 Draw me, we will run after thee: the king hath brought me into his chambers: we will be glad and rejoice in thee, we will remember thy love more than wine: the upright love thee.

1:5 I am black, but comely, O ye daughters of Jerusalem, as the tents of Kedar, as the curtains of Solomon.

1:6 Look not upon me, because I am black, because the sun hath looked upon me: my mother's children were angry with me; they made me the keeper of the vineyards; but mine own vineyard have I not kept.

1:7 Tell me, O thou whom my soul loveth, where thou feedest, where thou makest thy flock to rest at noon:

Let him kiss me with the kisses of his mouth:
for thy love is better than wine.

for why should I be as one that turneth aside by the flocks of thy companions?

1:8 If thou know not, O thou fairest among women, go thy way forth by the footsteps of the flock, and feed thy kids beside the shepherds' tents.

1:9 I have compared thee, O my love, to a company of horses in Pharaoh's chariots.

1:10 Thy cheeks are comely with rows of jewels, thy neck with chains of gold.

1:11 We will make thee borders of gold with studs of silver.

1:12 While the king sitteth at his table, my spikenard sendeth forth the smell thereof.

1:13 A bundle of myrrh is my well-beloved unto me; he shall lie all night betwixt my breasts.

1:14 My beloved is unto me as a cluster of camphire in the vineyards of Engedi.

1:15 Behold, thou art fair, my love; behold, thou art fair; thou hast doves' eyes.

1:16 Behold, thou art fair, my beloved, yea, pleasant: also our bed is green.

1:17 The beams of our house are cedar, and our rafters of fir.

I have compared thee, O my love,
to a company of horses in Pharaoh's chariots.

2

I am the rose of Sharon, and the lily of the valleys.

2:2 As the lily among thorns, so is my love among the daughters.

2:3 As the apple tree among the trees of the wood, so is my beloved among the sons. I sat down under his shadow with great delight, and his fruit was sweet to my taste.

2:4 He brought me to the banqueting house, and his banner over me was love.

2:5 Stay me with flagons, comfort me with apples: for I am sick of love.

2:6 His left hand is under my head, and his right hand doth embrace me.

2:7 I charge you, O ye daughters of Jerusalem, by the roes, and by the hinds of the field, that ye stir not up, nor awake my love, till he please.

2:8 The voice of my beloved! behold, he cometh leaping upon the mountains, skipping upon the hills.

2:9 My beloved is like a roe or a young hart: behold, he standeth behind our wall, he looketh forth at the windows, shewing himself through the lattice.

2:10 My beloved spake, and said unto me, Rise up, my love, my fair one, and come away.

2:11 For, lo, the winter is past, the rain is over and gone;

2:12 The flowers appear on the earth; the time of the singing of birds is come, and the voice of the turtle is heard in our land;

2:13 The fig tree putteth forth her green figs, and the vines with the tender grape give a good smell. Arise, my love, my fair one, and come away.

2:14 O my dove, that art in the clefts of the rock, in the secret places of the stairs, let me see thy countenance, let me hear thy voice; for sweet is thy voice, and thy countenance is comely.

2:15 Take us the foxes, the little foxes, that spoil the vines: for our vines have tender grapes.

2:16 My beloved is mine, and I am his: he feedeth among the lilies.

2:17 Until the day break, and the shadows flee away, turn, my beloved, and be thou like a roe or a young hart upon the mountains of Bether.

My beloved spake, and said unto me,
Rise up, my love, my fair one, and come away...
The flowers appear on the earth.

By night on my bed I sought him
whom my soul loveth:
I sought him, but I found him not.

3

By night on my bed I sought him whom my soul loveth: I sought him, but I found him not.

3:2 I will rise now, and go about the city in the streets, and in the broad ways I will seek him whom my soul loveth: I sought him, but I found him not.

3:3 The watchmen that go about the city found me: to whom I said, Saw ye him whom my soul loveth?

3:4 It was but a little that I passed from them, but I found him whom my soul loveth: I held him, and would not let him go, until I had brought him into my mother's house, and into the chamber of her that conceived me.

3:5 I charge you, O ye daughters of Jerusalem, by the roes, and by the hinds of the field, that ye stir not up, nor awake my love, till he please.

3:6 Who is this that cometh out of the wilderness like pillars of smoke, perfumed with myrrh and frankincense, with all powders of the merchant?

I will rise now, and go about the city in the streets,
and in the broad ways I will seek him whom my soul loveth.

3:7 Behold his bed, which is Solomon's; threescore valiant men are about it, of the valiant of Israel.

3:8 They all hold swords, being expert in war: every man hath his sword upon his thigh because of fear in the night.

3:9 King Solomon made himself a chariot of the wood of Lebanon.

3:10 He made the pillars thereof of silver, the bottom thereof of gold, the covering of it of purple, the midst thereof being paved with love, for the daughters of Jerusalem.

3:11 Go forth, O ye daughters of Zion, and behold king Solomon with the crown wherewith his mother crowned him in the day of his espousals, and in the day of the gladness of his heart. bucklers, all shields of mighty men.

Thou hast doves' eyes within thy locks:
thy hair is as a flock of goats.

4

Behold, thou art fair, my love; behold, thou art fair; thou hast doves' eyes within thy locks: thy hair is as a flock of goats, that appear from mount Gilead.

4:2 Thy teeth are like a flock of sheep that are even shorn, which came up from the washing; whereof every one bear twins, and none is barren among them.

4:3 Thy lips are like a thread of scarlet, and thy speech is comely: thy temples are like a piece of a pomegranate within thy locks.

4:4 Thy neck is like the tower of David builded for an armoury, whereon there hang a thousand bucklers, all shields of mighty men.

4:5 Thy two breasts are like two young roes that are twins, which feed among the lilies.

4:6 Until the day break, and the shadows flee away, I will get me to the mountain of myrrh, and to the hill of frankincense.

4:7 Thou art all fair, my love; there is no spot in thee.

4:8 Come with me from Lebanon, my spouse, with me from Lebanon: look from the top of Amana, from the top of Shenir and Hermon, from the lions' dens, from the mountains of the leopards.

4:9 Thou hast ravished my heart, my sister, my spouse; thou hast ravished my heart with one of thine eyes, with one chain of thy neck.

4:10 How fair is thy love, my sister, my spouse! how much better is thy love than wine! and the smell of thine ointments than all spices!

4:11 Thy lips, O my spouse, drop as the honeycomb: honey and milk are under thy tongue; and the smell of thy garments is like the smell of Lebanon.

4:12 A garden inclosed is my sister, my spouse; a spring shut up, a fountain sealed.

4:13 Thy plants are an orchard of pomegranates, with pleasant fruits; camphire, with spikenard,

4:14 Spikenard and saffron; calamus and cinnamon, with all trees of frankincense; myrrh and aloes, with all the chief spices:

4:15 A fountain of gardens, a well of living waters, and streams from Lebanon.

4:16 Awake, O north wind; and come, thou south; blow upon my garden, that the spices thereof may flow out. Let my beloved come into his garden, and eat his pleasant fruits.

5

I AM COME INTO MY GARDEN, MY SISTER, MY SPOUSE: I
have gathered my myrrh with my spice; I have eaten
my honeycomb with my honey; I have drunk my wine
with my milk: eat, O friends; drink, yea, drink abun-
dantly, O beloved.

5:2 I sleep, but my heart waketh: it is the voice of my
beloved that knocketh, saying, Open to me, my sister,
my love, my dove, my undefiled: for my head is filled
with dew, and my locks with the drops of the night.

5:3 I have put off my coat; how shall I put it on? I have
washed my feet; how shall I defile them?

5:4 My beloved put in his hand by the hole of the door,
and my bowels were moved for him.

5:5 I rose up to open to my beloved; and my hands
dropped with myrrh, and my fingers with sweet
smelling myrrh, upon the handles of the lock.

5:6 I opened to my beloved; but my beloved had

withdrawn himself, and was gone: my soul failed when he spake: I sought him, but I could not find him; I called him, but he gave me no answer.

5:7 The watchmen that went about the city found me, they smote me, they wounded me; the keepers of the walls took away my veil from me.

5:8 I charge you, O daughters of Jerusalem, if ye find my beloved, that ye tell him, that I am sick of love.

5:9 What is thy beloved more than another beloved, O thou fairest among women? what is thy beloved more than another beloved, that thou dost so charge us?

5:10 My beloved is white and ruddy, the chiefest among ten thousand.

5:11 His head is as the most fine gold, his locks are bushy, and black as a raven.

5:12 His eyes are as the eyes of doves by the rivers of waters, washed with milk, and fitly set.

5:13 His cheeks are as a bed of spices, as sweet flowers: his lips like lilies, dropping sweet smelling myrrh.

5:14 His hands are as gold rings set with the beryl: his belly is as bright ivory overlaid with sapphires.

5:15 His legs are as pillars of marble, set upon sockets of fine gold: his countenance is as Lebanon, excellent as the cedars.

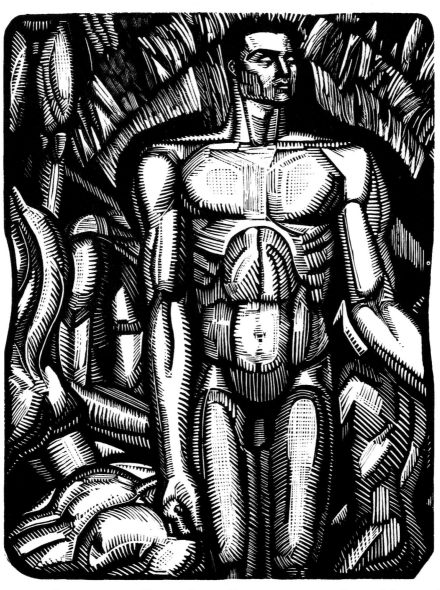

His legs are as pillars of marble, set upon sockets of fine gold:
his countenance is as Lebanon, excellent as the cedars.

5:16 His mouth is most sweet: yea, he is altogether lovely. This is my beloved, and this is my friend, O daughters of Jerusalem.

6

WHITHER IS THY BELOVED GONE, O THOU FAIREST AMONG women? whither is thy beloved turned aside? that we may seek him with thee.

6:2 My beloved is gone down into his garden, to the beds of spices, to feed in the gardens, and to gather lilies.

6:3 I am my beloved's, and my beloved is mine: he feedeth among the lilies.

6:4 Thou art beautiful, O my love, as Tirzah, comely as Jerusalem, terrible as an army with banners.

6:5 Turn away thine eyes from me, for they have overcome me: thy hair is as a flock of goats that appear from Gilead.

6:6 Thy teeth are as a flock of sheep which go up from the washing, whereof every one beareth twins, and there is not one barren among them.

6:7 As a piece of a pomegranate are thy temples within thy locks.

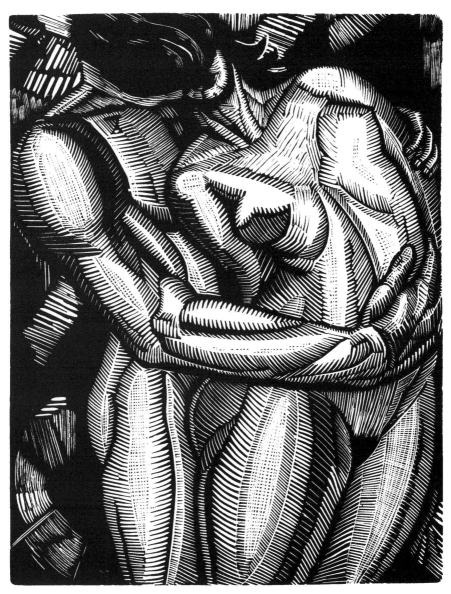

I *am my beloved's, and my beloved is mine:*
he feedeth among the lilies.

6:8 There are threescore queens, and fourscore concubines, and virgins without number.

6:9 My dove, my undefiled is but one; she is the only one of her mother, she is the choice one of her that bare her. The daughters saw her, and blessed her; yea, the queens and the concubines, and they praised her.

6:10 Who is she that looketh forth as the morning, fair as the moon, clear as the sun, and terrible as an army with banners?

6:11 I went down into the garden of nuts to see the fruits of the valley, and to see whether the vine flourished and the pomegranates budded.

6:12 Or ever I was aware, my soul made me like the chariots of Amminadib.

6:13 Return, return, O Shulamite; return, return, that we may look upon thee. What will ye see in the Shulamite? As it were the company of two armies.

7

How beautiful are thy feet with shoes, O prince's daughter! the joints of thy thighs are like jewels, the work of the hands of a cunning workman.

7:2 Thy navel is like a round goblet, which wanteth not liquor: thy belly is like an heap of wheat set about with lilies.

7:3 Thy two breasts are like two young roes that are twins.

7:4 Thy neck is as a tower of ivory; thine eyes like the fishpools in Heshbon, by the gate of Bathrabbim: thy nose is as the tower of Lebanon which looketh toward Damascus.

7:5 Thine head upon thee is like Carmel, and the hair of thine head like purple; the king is held in the galleries.

7:6 How fair and how pleasant art thou, O love, for delights!

7:7 This thy stature is like to a palm tree, and thy breasts to clusters of grapes.

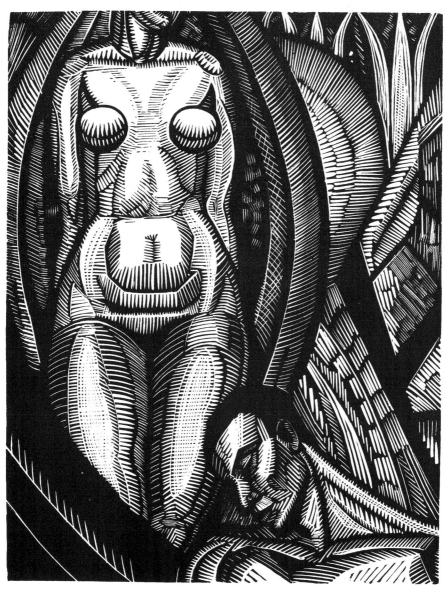

How fair and how pleasant art thou, O love, for delights!
This thy stature is like to a palm tree,
and thy breasts to clusters of grapes.

7:8 I said, I will go up to the palm tree, I will take hold of the boughs thereof: now also thy breasts shall be as clusters of the vine, and the smell of thy nose like apples;

7:9 And the roof of thy mouth like the best wine for my beloved, that goeth down sweetly, causing the lips of those that are asleep to speak.

7:10 I am my beloved's, and his desire is toward me.

7:11 Come, my beloved, let us go forth into the field; let us lodge in the villages.

7:12 Let us get up early to the vineyards; let us see if the vine flourish, whether the tender grape appear, and the pomegranates bud forth: there will I give thee my loves.

7:13 The mandrakes give a smell, and at our gates are all manner of pleasant fruits, new and old, which I have laid up for thee, O my beloved.

8

O THAT THOU WERT AS MY BROTHER, THAT SUCKED THE breasts of my mother! when I should find thee without, I would kiss thee; yea, I should not be despised.

8:2 I would lead thee, and bring thee into my mother's house, who would instruct me: I would cause thee to drink of spiced wine of the juice of my pomegranate.

8:3 His left hand should be under my head, and his right hand should embrace me.

8:4 I charge you, O daughters of Jerusalem, that ye stir not up, nor awake my love, until he please.

8:5 Who is this that cometh up from the wilderness, leaning upon her beloved? I raised thee up under the apple tree: there thy mother brought thee forth: there she brought thee forth that bare thee.

8:6 Set me as a seal upon thine heart, as a seal upon thine arm: for love is strong as death; jealousy is cruel as the grave: the coals thereof are coals of fire, which hath a most vehement flame.

Set me as a seal upon thine heart, as a seal upon thine arm:
for love is strong as death.

8:7 Many waters cannot quench love, neither can the floods drown it: if a man would give all the substance of his house for love, it would utterly be contemned.

8:8 We have a little sister, and she hath no breasts: what shall we do for our sister in the day when she shall be spoken for?

8:9 If she be a wall, we will build upon her a palace of silver: and if she be a door, we will inclose her with boards of cedar.

8:10 I am a wall, and my breasts like towers: then was I in his eyes as one that found favour.

8:11 Solomon had a vineyard at Baalhamon; he let out the vineyard unto keepers; every one for the fruit thereof was to bring a thousand pieces of silver.

8:12 My vineyard, which is mine, is before me: thou, O Solomon, must have a thousand, and those that keep the fruit thereof two hundred.

8:13 Thou that dwellest in the gardens, the companions hearken to thy voice: cause me to hear it.

8:14 Make haste, my beloved, and be thou like to a roe or to a young hart upon the mountains of spices.

The Voices

The Song of Songs is a conversation. There are three voices:

The woman
Her beloved
Their companions, who form a sort of chorus

Here is the order in which they speak:

1:2	*The woman*
1:4	*The chorus: "We will be glad…"*
1:5	*The woman*
1:8	*The man*
1:12	*The woman*
1:15	*The man*
1:16	*The woman*
1:17	*The man*
2:1	*The woman*
2:2	*The man*
2:3	*The woman*
2:13	*The man*

2:16 The woman

4:1   The man
4:16 The woman

5:1   The man
5:2   The woman
5:9   The chorus
5:10 The woman

6:1   The chorus
6:2   The woman
6:4   The man
6:11 The woman
6:13 The chorus
      The man: "What will ye see?"

7:9   The woman

8:5   The chorus
      The woman: "I raised thee up…"
8:8   The chorus
8:10 The woman
8:13 The man
8:14 The woman

Cecil Buller

Cecil Buller

An appreciation by her son, Sean B. Murphy

CECIL BULLER WAS BORN IN MONTREAL, CANADA IN 1886. HER FATHER was Dr. Frank Buller, a prominent ophthalmologist who became the first specialist in the Faculty of Medicine at McGill University. He encouraged her to study art and develop her artistic skills.

The Song of Solomon woodcuts are a milestone in my mother's distinguished career. She was a modernist artist well ahead of her time. To understand how this work came into being, it is important to look at her career and the influences that shaped her art.

Her first teacher was the well known painter William Brymner at the Art Association of Montreal (later the Montreal Museum of Fine Arts). He emphasized figure drawing, and this interest remained with her all her life.

After two years of study, Brymner told her he could not teach her anything more and recommended she go to Paris to continue her studies. There she studied with Maurice Denis and was exposed to the art of Monet, Renoir, Gaugin, Cézanne and others. It was Cézanne and Denis in particular who influenced her.

In 1917 she married the American artist John J.A. Murphy, who helped her decide the direction her work was to take. They had met at the London Central School of Art and Design in 1916 as students of Noel Rooke.

Rooke taught printmaking, and emphasized that woodcuts were a distinct art form. It followed that Cecil Buller and her husband became enthusiastic and dedicated woodcut artists.

The *Song of Solomon* series was published in Paris in 1931 in a limited edition of 80 copies by Éditions du Raisin, Maurice Darantière's press. It was accompanied by Isaac de Maistre de Sacy's (1613–1684) 1672 French translation of the *Cantique des cantiques* from the *Vulgate*. The typography and layout were designed by her husband. The present publication in English uses the King James version of the *Bible*.

Cecil Buller loved life and beauty. The eleven prints are powerful and full of passion. They celebrate the relationship of man and woman and man and woman in nature. The last print in the 1931 edition (p 12 here) daringly places the lovers amidst the skyscrapers of New York City.

Work of this strength with its emphasis on the figure and its placement in the luxuriance of nature was unusual in the 1920's and early 1930's.

Cecil Buller was a woman of passion who enjoyed close friendships. She loved parties, had a wonderful sense of humor, and enjoyed being with an eclectic group of friends that included artists, writers and politicians. She was a great traveller. While she lived mainly in New York and Montreal, she felt especially at home in Paris.

At the same time, she required hours of solitude to produce her work. She made untold numbers of sketches prior to drawing in black and white ink on the hard boxwood block. Only then could the demanding cutting begin. She printed all her own woodcuts by carefully pressing the paper over the inked block with a large spoon. Any prints that did not meet her high standards were discarded. She was a lifelong perfectionist.

The Song of Solomon shows her emphasis on the figure and the importance of drawing. Its strong lyrical quality relates to her experience in Paris. It was a happy time in her life.

Later on, and especially after World War II the work was to become more philosophical, reflecting the anxieties felt by human beings caught in the uncertainties of the postwar era. She died in 1973.

Cecil Buller summed up her feelings about life when, at her request, her tombstone was inscribed, "She loved beauty."

Sean B. Murphy

Sean B. Murphy

This book was designed by Douglas McKercher
and published in Ottawa, Canada
by the Fomorian Press, November 2000.
The text typeface is 18 pt AGFA Cartier.